Introduction

Mastery and Your Life

Are you living your ideal life, right now?

Whether you are or you are not, can you rate yourself a 10+ on having a great life, being satisfied with who you are as a person, what you've accomplished, and what you've contributed back to the world?

Or do you still have unfulfilled dreams and ambitions that perhaps you are procrastinating on?

Many people I've asked, say they've never even thought about what they really want in life. They are so busy in their day-to-day life that they don't even think to step back and ask,

"Hmmm… is my life going in the direction I want it to? Will I have regrets when I'm 103?"

Without clear goals in life, it's no wonder money is used to try and satisfy that underlying discontentment. It's no wonder the unhappiness and blame are taken out on relationships.

Discovering the cause of any underlying unhappiness about the way your life is headed, is critical.

You are the only person in charge of your life.

Introduction

Mastery and Your Life

Without clear goals and a willingness to take charge of your life, you end up by default, following others' ideals. Often relationships, careers, and/or lifestyles end up where they are because you did what you "should" do. Being too scared to end an unhealthy relationship, or too nervous to change careers, or too insecure to say 'no' to buying that new home…all of these fears keep you stuck, following what other people think a great life is. But what about you?

Why not master your own life?

You may be thinking, "Of course! Of course I master my life. I am who I am, and I'm proud of it!" And maybe you are. And I'm sure there's lots to be proud of. But is there part of you who's hiding behind the idea that maybe you've come to accept this is what life dealt you, so you'd better make the most of it?

This is an attitude of defeat. Not to mention being a victim, instead of a warrior.

Introduction

Mastery and Your Life

The Bhagavad Gita, a classic of Indian philosophy, points to these very qualities for the warrior on the battlefield.

> Heroism, power, determination, resourcefulness, courage in battle, generosity and leadership are the natural qualities of work for the warriors. 18.43

Not fleeing the battlefield is the <u>duty</u> of the warrior!

What's your duty?

What responsibility do you have for your life?

Certainly it takes heroism, power, determination, resourcefulness, courage and leadership to take charge of your life.

You cannot delegate the responsibility for your life.

You, and only you, can fulfill the duty of creating a sustainable, fulfilling, satisfying life. It is your duty to listen to your heart's desires, listen to your true nature, and follow the guidance that is provided.

On success...

Success & Mastery

So, what is success, anyway?

Well, guess what? YOU get to determine what success is. YOU define success. Once you are clear on what will make you successful, then you can take actions.

In Sanskrit, the word **jayah** जयः means mastery As you become aware and awake to your actions you gain mastery.

But my favorite definition of success is:

"Taking steps toward a worthwhile goal."

This definition is valuable, because you only have to do two things to be successful.

1) you must have worthwhile goals, and
2) you must take steps toward them.

That's it.

Actually attaining your goals, and achieving what you desire, is fun and rewarding. But what if you never make it?

There will be factors outside of your control that may determine the course and outcome of your efforts. But the diligence and gratification of staying on track will far outweigh the relief of quitting when you are defeated.

On success...

Success & Mastery

Whether in your relationship or looking at success with your money, the hard part will be to actually follow through on your action steps.

And this is where mastery is important. It takes:

COURAGE,

DETERMINATION

and a sheer

DESIRE FOR SUCCESS

to face your fears and venture into the unknown. This is **abhaya** अभय, fearlessness!

And yes, you will have to make changes in your life that you KNOW will improve your health, happiness and relationships, and those changes will not be easy.

However, mastery has little to do with being easy! It has more to do with continuing to improve yourself, facing difficulties, and moving forward anyway.

There are stages of growth and maturity that you will discover as you head down the road to mastering your life, relationships and your money. And as you progress, you will feel terrible at times, and feel elated at others...this is the road to mastery.

On mastery…

What is Mastery?

Definition of Master *\verb*

- Acquire complete knowledge or skill in an accomplishment, technique, or art
- Gain control of; overcome
- Become eminently skilled in something

Mastery is dedicating yourself
to excellence in a particular area.

In modern times, it is difficult to master one particular thing, because there are so many options available. Our culture has created so many options and opportunities that we've become accustomed quit, and try something new when it gets tough.

Mastery means staying consistent in your efforts even when it's hard, and using those difficulties to become even greater.

When it comes to relationships, it's easy to get divorced when it's difficult. When it comes to wealth, it's easy to succumb to the temptations of the immediate desires and forego the long-term gratification.

On mastery...

So why do we take the easy road, more often then facing the challenges of mastery?

Because we are bombarded with messages of comfort, "feel good", laziness and relaxation.

The cultural influence states that we are 'on the right track' when things feel good. That sends the message that when things hurt or are uncomfortable, it must mean you are doing something wrong.

"When you are doing things wrong,

then doing things right, feels wrong." J. Griggs

Were you taught in your upbringing the discipline, determination, dedication necessary to stick through the hard parts and continue the path of mastery? For most of us, the answer is NO.

In the Principles of Mastery, you will recognize the point at which you tend to quit. It may be different for each person, but as I go through

the stages and the 14 Principles of Mastery, look for the point in time that you habitually quit your endeavors. Ask yourself, "what has kept me from moving past this?"

That question will uncover your weaknesses so that you can overcome them and stay on the road to mastery in your life, relationships, and your money.

On mastery…

Why is Mastery Important ?

Yes, you can apply mastery to relationships, money, arts, sciences, music, careers, and many other aspects of life.

However the underlying, and most important type of mastery, is self-mastery.

WHY IS SELF-MASTERY SO IMPORTANT?

Self-mastery is gaining complete knowledge of, gaining control over, and becoming eminently skilled in… YOU!

This entails a dedicated practice of self-inquiry and actions in your thoughts, attitudes and behaviors.

Most people do not obtain mastery in any endeavor in life because they are not willing to go through the tedious stages of perfection and precision necessary to gain mastery.

Most people quit when it gets hard, looking only for the 'lure' and fun of mastery, rather than the satisfaction of consistently performing the grueling work that it takes to truly master anything.

On mastery…

Why is Mastery Important ?

Most are anxious to get to the next level without spending the required time on the fundamentals.

When you try and skip to higher levels of mastery without diligence in the basics; you are only rebelling!

This is often seen when students act as though they know more than their teacher, try to make changes in the organization without understanding the bigger picture, or try to teach others when they have not yet mastered it themselves. Eventually they end up quitting.

When you stick with it and learn new fundamentals, you can move along the road of mastery. On this road, you gain a mature, self-aware perspective, and can begin to take 100% responsibility for your life and drop all blame of others and outside experiences.

And when each of us does this, we will see more peace, freedom, and generosity in our relationships, communities, nations and the world as a whole.

On money...

Money and Mastery

So when it comes to money, why is it, that no matter how much money you have or don't have, you still find yourself in discontentment or perhaps even misery?

Its seems like PEACE flies right out the door when it comes to money.

Money is still associated with survival.

It triggers a primal reaction (and not always a rational reaction) when threatened.

It's so easy to think that having a lot of money will solve life's struggles and give you instant freedom.

But that is not the case.

Having money offers you lots of things, and freedom as well, but it doesn't offer you peace. **Peace comes from mastery, not acquisitions.**

Over the years in my career as a CPA, Financial Planner, Money Coach and Entrepreneur, I began to notice some patterns that were holding my clients back from making the personal progress they wanted to make.

On money...

Money and Mastery

One of the most significant patterns I saw was the lack of desire to look at money.

Many clients, associates, friends, and peers just hate looking at their money or even talking about it.

This is because they don't know how to address it without those primal fears coming up.

Whether it's **fear, embarrassment, shame, or trying to avoid a fight**....all of these emotions kept them from looking at the numbers and trying to understand their money.

Mastery of money and of your self, gives you not only the detachment from your reaction, but also allows you to see money more objectively.

Specifically, it allows you to make better decisions, to become happier, and to use money to bring your relationships closer together.

On relationships…

Relationships and Mastery

Is it possible to use money to bring relationships closer together, instead of tearing them apart?

Of course!

Imagine…having shared goals

Imagine…creating a plan together

Imagine…talking about money

Imagine…taking vacations together

Imagine…growing your wealth together

Mastery in your relationship means to obtain complete knowledge of, gain control over, and become eminently skilled in… RELATING TO EACH OTHER!

This means being able to listen, understand, have a desire to work together and committing to 100% responsibility.

TO GAIN MASTERY IN YOUR RELATIONSHIP, YOU MUST START WITH SELF-MASTERY.

The stages and Principles of Mastery are a process of growing up. They take you from beginner to expert, so you CAN have what you want in life and your relationships.

The wise…

Tapping into Ancient Wisdom

If it weren't for my instructor, Sensei Cogen Bohanec, I would have no way to connect the dots between my understanding of mastery and that of the ancient principles in martial arts and Sanskrit philosophies.

Sensei Bohanec is a graduate level student of Sanksrit and Asian Studies at UC Berkeley, as well as a third degree black-belt in Shotokan Karate. (www.sonomayogamartialarts.com)

His dream of bridging the gap between martial arts and these ancient philosophies has inspired me to tie these concepts to how we use money in life and in our relationships…

and discover true freedom.

Through many hours of study with him, and with his guidance in creating this booklet, Sensei Bohanec has lead me to various resources of ancient concepts that I am applying to these Principles of Mastery.

The wise…

Tapping into Ancient Wisdom

The objective of this booklet is to tie together the wisdom of over 2000 years ago, to the current principles of mastery that you can employ in your daily life.

My curiosity of why Karate is about non-violence brought me to studying not just the Karate principles, but now a craving for much more knowledge and a deeper understanding of principles that humans have been questing for since the beginning of time (which before I started practicing Karate, I had NO idea about the principles and 'way of life' that any martial art offers).

The roots of Karate are primarily Zen of which can be traced even further back to the Yoga Sutras. And even the Yoga Sutras come during a period of philosophical discovery which are linked in major texts such as the Bhagavad Gita and the Vedas.

In this booklet, I am tapping into the resources of these ancient philosophies:

- The Patanjali Yoga Sutras
- The Bhagavad Gita
- Shotokan Karate's Dojo and Niju Kun
- Zen Buddhism

to bring you concepts that relate to modern day thoughts on self-mastery.

Stages of Growth

Before we enter into the 14 Principles of Mastery, let me introduce to you the bigger picture of what transpires when you take the journey from ordinary to mastery.

The first stage that you encounter is that of FORCING. In this stage, you will find that it takes rigorous effort, strong will, and high motivation to keep going.

But as you gain some skills and your body and mind adjust, you can begin to start RELEASING your efforts and exploring a new perspective.

As you maintain your consistent practice and become dedicated to your mastery, you will begin to let go, and start ALLOWING the principles to work through you automatically.

As you reach the final stages, you begin to feel the pull and responsibility to share what you've learned.

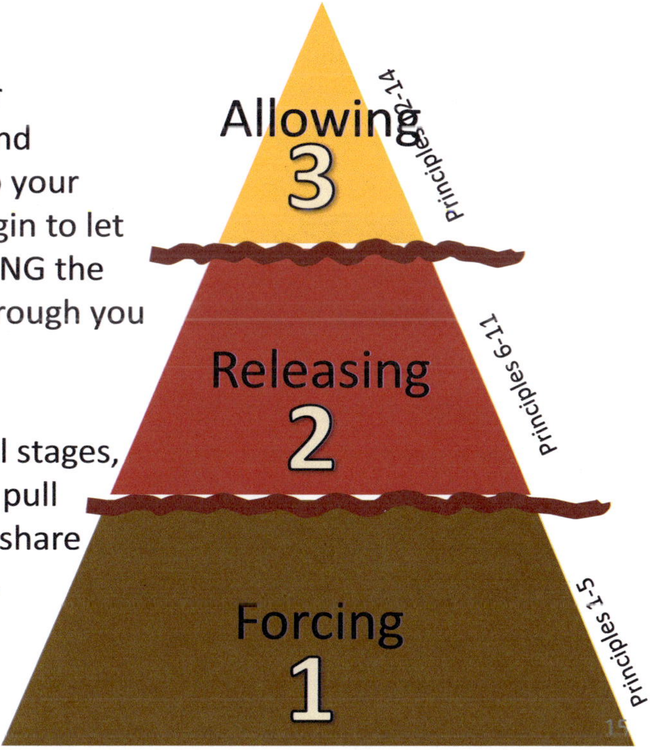

14 Principles of Mastery

In my own journey of mastery and the many years of study and inquiry, I've identified the layers of learning that happen as you begin to make changes in your life. With each layer is a new principle that brings the necessary skills, attitudes and willingness, that allow you to be ready to move along to the next principle.

These 14 Principles appear when you are trying to make new changes in your diet, relationships, money, exercise, careers, or any other area of your life. They take you through the transformation needed to become a master.

1. Despise Your Current Condition
2. Willingness to Begin
3. Trust the Teacher
4. Apply Intense Effort
5. Determination
6. Commitment
7. Discover a Bigger Purpose
8. Self-Inquiry
9. Relaxation
10. Effect on Surroundings
11. Independence of Teacher
12. Integration Into Your Life
13. Self-Surrender
14. Give Back/Teach Others

14 PRINCIPLES OF MASTERY

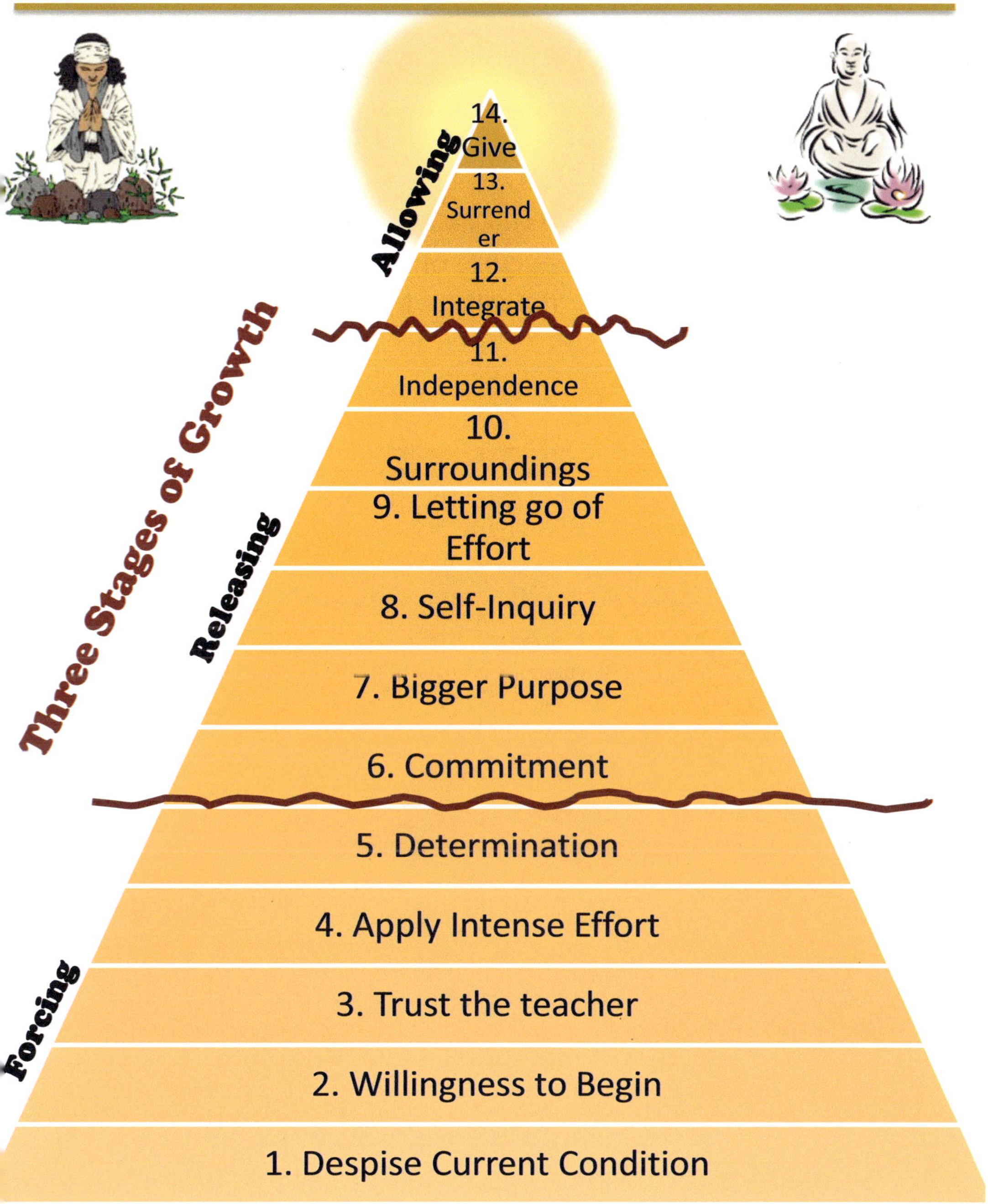

PRINCIPLES 1-5

STAGE 1: FORCING

The first stage is that of FORCING your efforts. Principles 1-5 each fall into this category of rigorous effort, strong will, and high motivation to keep going.

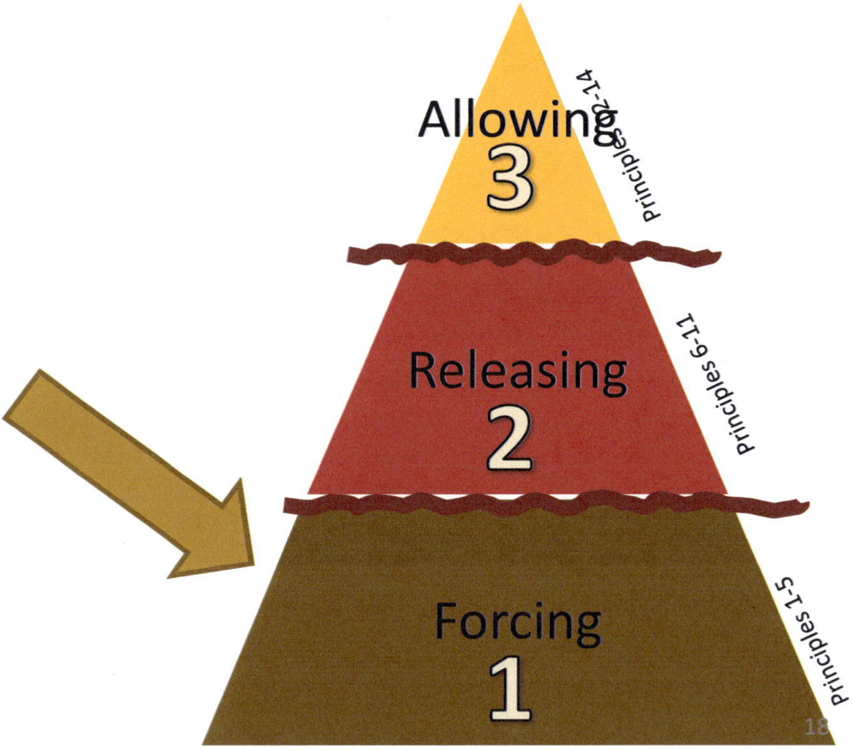

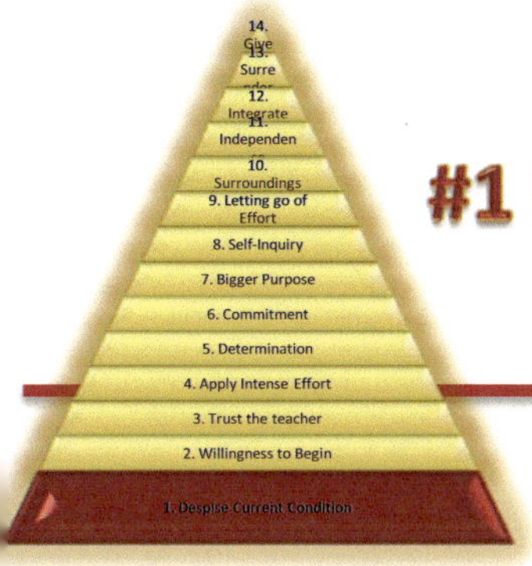

#1 Despise Your Current Situation

To start a new journey in your life and hitting the road to mastery, something must propel you to get started. Being a beginner, starting new habits, and trying new things is scary and unpredictable and few people make the decision to change without resistance.

So in order to take the leap, you will get to the point where you've had enough! You may get frustrated, worn out, hopeless and **'sick and tired of being sick and tired'** in your current situation.

But this is GOOD! Get mad! Despise your situation and your role in it! Gain intolerance for its unhealthiness and face the reality of its destruction. This is where motivation and drive will plant the seeds of success.

A key focus of the Zen teaching is the Four Noble Truths, and the first is the doctrine of **dukha** (suffering). Most people don't want to look at the bad, but in Buddhism, facing the truth of what causes pain and suffering is critical. Pain comes from **trishna** (craving). Either clinging to desire (**raga**), avoiding the undesirable (**dvesha**) or wanting things to be different than the way there (**avidya**).

In Indic philosophy the term **rajas** (motion, energy, excitement) describes the passion and energy needed to push through and take action. An increase in rajas must be present to fuel that desire to get out of the current state. When rajas outweighs **tamas** (lethargy), motivation and drive ensue. To bring in more **sattvic** energy will allow to experience a balance between the two.

#2 Willingness to Begin

Readiness begins when you have felt the pain long enough and are finally ready to make a change. All of your efforts to this point have been futile and as of now, you are not capable of achieving what you want with the level of knowledge, skills, and experience that you have.

Admitting this takes humility.

It is time to be a beginner. It is time to surrender your old ways and find new ways that you don't know, understand, or trust yet.

This requires that you have faith in new philosophies, trust in new people and take steps into unknown and unfamiliar territories..

The Japanese word **shoshin** (beginner's mind), is a Zen term often used in martial arts to depict that state of mind necessary to become a humble student. It refers to having an attitude of openness, eagerness, and lack of preconceptions. Even a black belt must maintain a beginners mind to be able to learn and grow, just as if it were their first day in training.

The Bhagavad Gita is a classic of Indian spirituality. It is a metaphorical story of internal conflict, depicted on a battle field. **Arjuna** (the warrior), cries to Krishna (his Lord) in verse 2.07 "My will is paralyzed, and I am utterly confused. Tell me which is the better path for me... give me instruction." His plea is a demonstration of his humbleness and willingness to be lead.

#3 Trust the Teacher

Before you put your trust in someone you don't know, you must first put your faith (**shruddha** श्रुद्ध) in them. Trust comes from repeated actions and consistent results. If you want to build trust in your teacher/mentor, then you must first have faith in them. The faster you can gain trust in your teacher, the faster you will grow.

As you learn that your teacher has your best interest at heart, and you see repeated actions and results, then you can begin to build trust. This level of risk and faith is demonstrated through the humility and respect you show for him/her.

Shotokan Karate has 5 Dojo Kun, and 20 Niju Kun; the guiding principles of character for the martial artist. Niju Kun #1 **"Karate-do wa rei ni hajimari rei ni owaru koto a wasaru na"** (Karate begins with a bow and ends with a bow) displays respect not only to the Sensei, but to the art, and the students. It emphasizes the importance of treating everyone with equal respect. "Respect must be DEMONSTRATED, otherwise it is as if it doesn't exist."

In most philosophies, there's a formula for discovering truth. In Yoga, truth (or right knowledge) **pramana**, is determined by 1) your direct experience (**pratyaksha**), 2) your logical deductive reasoning (**anumana**) and 3) your reliance on credible sources (**agamah**). Learning how to discern <u>what</u> to trust is a critical element for a beginner.

#4 Apply Intense Effort

As you begin the journey down a new road and start putting in the effort to learn new skills, this is the time that all your resistance arises. Your old habits try to pull you back to the ‘norm’ of old ways; and it takes tremendous effort to stay on the new path.

It’s no different than hiking a big mountain. When hiking, the first sight of becoming winded and tired, you’ll want to turn around and go back, and/or sit down and rest. However...

this is NOT the time to rest or retreat!

This is the time to use intense effort (**virya वीर्य**), and push through that resistance. Force yourself to keep going, even if everything in you wants to quit.

Dojo Kun #2, “**Makoto no michi o mamoru koto”** (Be faithful) means to do things even when you don’t want to. It is the struggle itself that develops you and your character. Niju Khun #7 “**Waza wai wa ketai ni seizu**” (Misfortune comes out of idleness) also points out that without effort, you will certainly face defeat and sloth that accompanies it.

In the Yoga Sutras (1.20-1.22) it states that there are prescribed practices and varying levels of intensity of those practices. However, Sutra 1.21 (**tivra samvega asannah**) points out that those who move quickly in their practice, with intensity and vigor will achieve their results more quickly. This focuses on the *speed* of the effort as well as the *intensity* of the effort.

#5 Show Pure Determination

When applying the intense effort of the previous Principle, you were using your efforts to get you going and push through the initial pain of getting started. But now you need to use your effort toward **NOT QUITTING.**

This is a different perspective, because now you must find determination. This is the point that you realize you will have to make changes in your lifestyle, your life situation, your relationships, etc. In the next Principle you will have to face the decision to commit to your new path, but right now, you begin to see how your life is deeply designed to keep you stuck in your old habits. Your single focused determination (**ekagrata** एकाग्रत) at this point will keep you going, and continue to raise the awareness of more changes to come.

Dojo Kun #3, "**Doryoku no seishin o yashinau koto**" (Endeavor) emphasizes the spirit of endurance. Endeavor means to always work toward your goals, even if you must make sacrifices elsewhere in your life. To endure means to continue moving forward, whether it's difficult or not and whether it hurts or not. Neither of these are relevant when it comes to the journey of mastery.

To gain mastery, one must begin restraining from distractions through consistent practice, **abhyasa,** and without interruption, **nairantarya** (1.14). To develop an unshakable practice, one cannot quit because they feel like it. It must be sustained **dirgha-kaala** (over a prolonged period of time).

PRINCIPLES 6-11

STAGE 2: RELEASING

As you begin to gain some skills and your body and mind adjust, you can begin to slow down on the intensity of your forcefulness, and start RELEASING your efforts and exploring a new perspective.

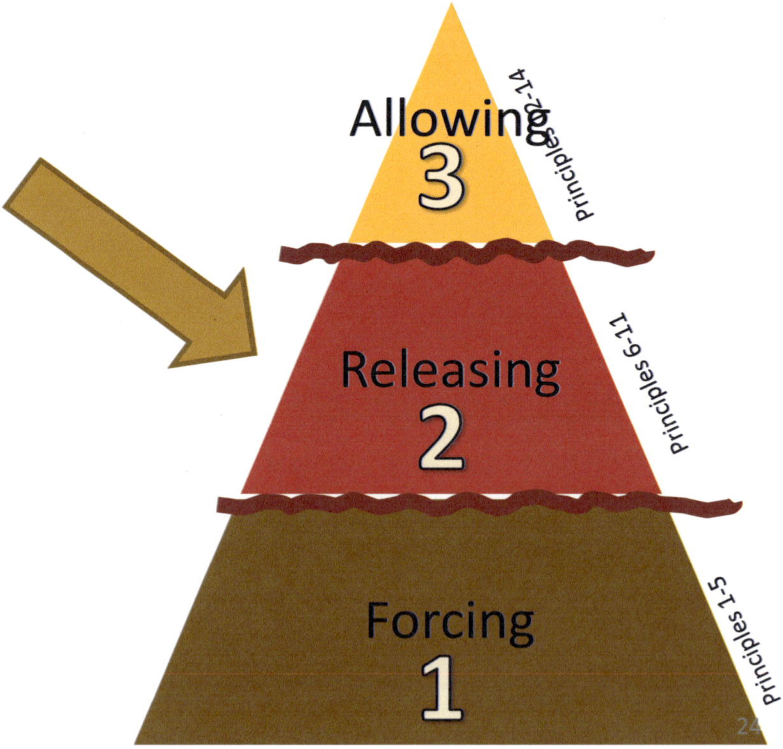

#6 Commitment to Longevity

At this point, it's time to move out of the FORCING stage, and into the RELEASING stage. The Principles shift from having to <u>effort</u> at each step, to letting go of the forcefulness . But in order to make the shift from FORCING to RELEASING, it takes a new level of trust. Not only must you rely more heavily on your teachers and mentors, now you must begin to trust yourself and your abilities.

But you are now faced with the choice...do you make the lifelong **commitment to mastery...or do you quit** and go back to your old ways?

Making the decision to become the new person you are striving for, is a lifelong commitment. **Are you ready for it?**

Niju Kun #11, "**Karate wa yu gotoshi taezu netsu o ataezareba moto no mizu ni kaeru**" (Karate is just like hot water; if you do not give it continuous heat, it will become cold) states that without a commitment to continuous practice and learning, you will lose what you have gained. You must apply DAILY practice to gain precision and learn new levels of skills.

In the Yoga Sutras (2.13), the Bhagavad Gita, Vedic traditions, as well as in Buddhism, the concept of **mah-vratam** (the great vow) is of highest importance. It is a vow to your highest virtues, non-violence being the highest. Yet, not a vow of perfection, but of a committed intention to give each moment your best effort toward honoring this vow of living your highest virtues.

#7 Discover a Bigger Purpose

As you continue to develop consistent practice and release effort, you will see a bigger perspective and purpose. Your efforts toward mastery are not just about you. Now is the time for you to get a glimpse of how your own personal achievement benefits others. You as an individual can bring a new perspective that allows for more generosity, compassion, love, maturity, cooperation, and a greater good to the world.

So WHY is it important to eliminate suffering and create a better world?

Each person must discover their own "why", but can you imagine what relationships, money, health and life would be like if suffering were reduced or eliminated?

"Seek perfection of character" **(jinkaku kansei ni tsutomuro koto)** is the first of the Dojo Kun. Martial arts are a way of living and character development that allows one to become a better person. This is what inspired my quest for an understanding of what martial arts is all about. Karate offers a higher purpose of developing the body, mind, soul and character of the practitioner, to make the person, hence the world, better.

Most spiritual philosophies have a purpose of realizing something bigger than you as an individual and to reduce suffering. Yoga Sutra 2.16, (**heyam duhkam anagatam**) says that suffering that has yet to manifest is to be avoided, which means that the most important (and the ONLY) type of suffering that we can stop is the future suffering that our current actions will bring.

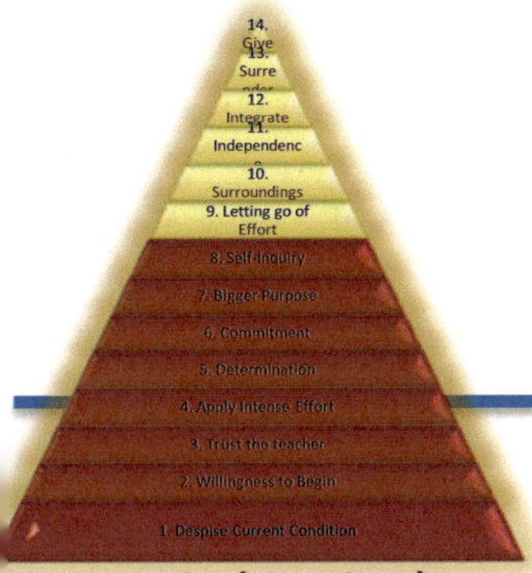

8 Focus on Self-Inquiry

True wisdom is the result of learning to inquire into yourself, your actions, your behaviors and your responses. It's not just looking objectively and seeing your strengths and weaknesses, it's the ability to adjust your life based on what you discover.

By using your personal inquiry to make corrections in your behavior, you will continue down the road of self-mastery and of character building. Self-inquiry gives you two important qualities:

1) responsibility for yourself, and **2) compassion and empathy** for others.

The better you know yourself the faster you can stop blaming others, have a greater impact on others, and start taking action in positive ways.

"Know yourself first, then you can know others", this is Niju Kun #4 **(mazu jiko o shire, shikoshite ta o shire).** Knowing yourself means knowing the difference between who you are striving to be, and who you are today. Knowing yourself allows you to see the strengths and weaknesses of others. The more you can see what's happening in **you**, the better you will be able to interact, respond, and relate with others.

Atma darshana means self-inquiry and in Yoga Sutra 2.41, Patanjali points out that by gaining mental purity, you can have a clearer vision of yourself. With that clarity comes the quieting of the mind **(chitta vritti nirodah)** and the ensuing stillness and liberation; the ultimate goal of yoga.

9 Letting Go of Effort

We've been talking about letting go of effort in several different ways, yet now there is a new level of letting go that is required. Until now you've been practicing your new skills diligently, you've made a commitment to your lifestyle, and now it's time to start trusting that what you've learned can be your automatic reaction, without your direct effort.

Still not yet a master, it's time to stop running every move through your rational mind, and start **allowing your body and words to act spontaneously**.

You will see that over-efforting will slow you down, inhibit your progress, and hold you back if you continue to "make" things happen. You must trust that all the hard work you've put in will now start to come naturally.

Kokoro wa hanatan koto o yosu : means "Be ready to release your mind" in Niju Kun #6. This is critical in order to be present, alert, and able to move according to the situation. If you are thinking about it, it's too late. Also, by filling your mind with new ideas, then releasing the effort, you have space to receive more. Having an empty mind means having an open mind.

Prayatna-saithilya means relaxation of effort and in Yoga Sutra 2.47, Patanjali notes that you can only attain the what you are trying to master by relaxing your effort. As you gradually slacken your effort your body and mind will adjust, but there comes a point that you must break the connection of effort in order to let it happen on its own.

#10 Your Affect on Your Surroundings

As you relax your efforts, you will begin to see (and maybe even for the first time) that <u>you</u> have a direct affect on your surroundings. Not only are the environment and people around you reacting to your words and actions; but you can now see with much more clarity what others are saying and doing. You become more aware of the impact you have.

The focus shifts from YOU…to others.

You have a direct influence on others and your environment. You are now becoming a leader and a role model to others who want to discover their own mastery. Your actions now reflect a greater impact without the personal conflict, and with a new found inner **PEACE**.

Sensei Bohanec always says, "react spontaneously to a situation AS it arises" and Niju Kun #13: **Teki ni yotte tenka seyo,** states "Move according to your opponent". Both of these require an empty mind and an acute awareness of what's happening around you and in others. To be able to act (or react) spontaneously, you must not be focused on YOU!

"Ahimsa-pratishthayam tat-samnidhau vairatyagah", Yoga Sutra 2.35, translates as "Being firmly established in non-violence there is abandonment of hostility in your presence." In other words, your mastery will have a direct affect on others. They will see, sense, and know that your commitment to peace and mastery is inspiring and liberating.

PRINCIPLES 11-14

STAGE 3: ALLOWING

As you maintain your consistent practice and become dedicated to your mastery, you will begin to let go, and start ALLOWING the principles to work through you automatically.

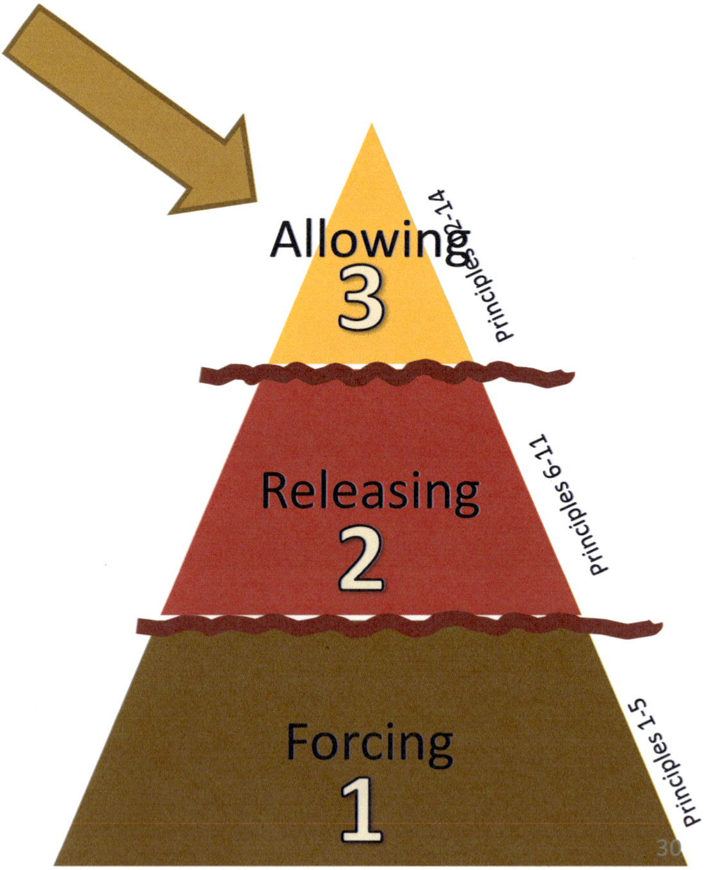

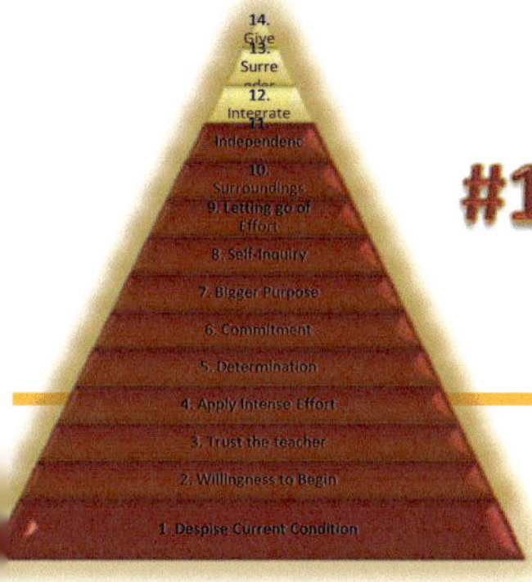

#11 Independence from Teacher

Now you are moving into the growth stage of ALLOWING, and surpassing the FORCING and RELEASING stages. Once you've mastered the correct application of the last stages, now you can start embracing the next three Principles of the ALLOWING stage. With the skill, the humbleness, and the readiness you've gained, you've built the foundation for lasting changes.

With these, you can now begin to explore your own application of your teachings. With a new independence you can **explore new ways of applying the skills you've gained** and discover ways to learn on your own.

As you explore on your own, you will gain a new level of understanding the concepts you've been practicing. But it is not something that can be given...you must reach out and take it now.

Niju Kun #20: **Tsune ni shinen kufu seyo,** states to "Always create and devise". The term **Sensei** means 'one who is experienced or has gone before', and your teacher/Sensei can never do the movement for you. You must learn to continually create and devise new applications of what you learn based on the situation at hand.

Jnana is the standard term for the highest kind of knowledge (wisdom), but not of book-learning; of direct knowledge and spiritual wisdom. The great yoga master, Ramakrishna, says, "one who has merely heard of fire has **ajnana** (ignorance). One who has seen fire has **jnana** (wisdom, experience, knowledge). But one who has actually built a fire and cooked on it has **vijnana** (practical application of knowledge).

#12 Integrate into Your Life

With all that you have gained through your studies and practices, it is time to integrate this wisdom into multiple areas of your life. For example, if you've gained mastery in communication in your relationships, these same Principles can be applied to your physical fitness, your diet, your money, your career, your leisure, your family, etc. Once you've gained them in one area, they can now be applied in others.

You've fundamentally changed who you are and now it's time to explore how that affects other aspects of your life.

Having guidelines, routines, and principles to live by make it easier to maintain consistency in your practice.

Niju Kun #10 says to "Put Karate into your everyday living...that is how to see its true beauty" **(Ara yuru mon o karateka seyo; soko ni myomi ari).**

In order to really appreciate true mastery, you must apply it everywhere. This is a change in your character. **Budo**, the Japanese word for martial arts, means "to stop conflict" and the conflict that must be stopped is the conflict within yourself.

Most philosophies have guidelines for living that bring personal happiness and self-mastery. In Yoga, it's the **Astangas** (2.29) (eight limbs) that are the prescription for liberation, where as in Zen, it's the Four Noble Truths, which include the Eightfold Path. These guidelines are examples from two philosophies of ancient times.

(see Appendix A & B)

#13 Self-Surrender

Self-surrender is the point that you decide to release your control and surrender to something greater than you. Whether you call it God, spirit, Ishvara, universe, or whatever term you are accustomed to, it's the time that you let go completely and allow the guidance from this God/spirit to provide you instructions for living a great life.

Not just instructions, but the courage to take action and follow that guidance.

And it's not to make YOU happier, but to gain a larger happiness, liberation, and reduced suffering for humanity and for the world as a whole.

Niju Kun #5 says "Spirit and mind are more important than technique" **(gijutsu yori shinjutsu).** This points out the importance of the development of **shinjitsu** (spiritual skill and development). Spiritual development means surrendering your 'self' or your ego, and allowing something greater than you to guide you.

In Yoga, the Sutras offer multiple ways of achieving spiritual liberation, but the quickest is through **"Ishvara-pranidhanad va"** (Sutra 1.23). Which means devotion to, or self-surrender to God. The emphasis here is not to surrender to one particular type of God/spirit, but that **self-surrender** is a faster way to obtain the willingness to receive and act upon the higher guidance and direction.

#14 Give Back & Teach Others

Obtaining the mastery and the precision of your new endeavor, you have a responsibility to give back to others. Just as any student, there comes a point where taking the knowledge that you have gained and applying it in life becomes a responsibility. If you remain a student forever, you hoard the information that someone else freely gave to you.

When you become an expert, a master, you must teach others or the knowledge and wisdom is wasted.

This takes courage to step out of the student role, and become the teacher, but it is necessary not only for others, but for your own continued learning.

In the Bhavagad Gita, there is a whole chapter on **karma-yoga** (action) or selfless service. In this chapter, the obligation of selfless action, action out of duty, is necessary not for the individual's sake, but for the welfare of all. It is the path of action without expectation or attachment to the outcome. In giving to the greater good, true liberation ensues.

Seva is an other form of selfless service. Seva is a combination of both **karma-yoga** (action) and **bhakti** (devotion). Sensei Bohanec describes being devoted as a higher obligation than of just making a commitment. Being devoted means giving one's time, energy, and focus entirely. Devoting yourself to mastery, means devoting your efforts to your continued efforts as well as helping others discover mastery as well.

How to start today...

Developing mastery in your money and in your relationships means taking the first step...that of being honest with your current situation. Taking an inventory of what's really going on.

Sensei Bohanec tells me all the time not to run from the anger or disappointment. In fact, "dive into it more", he says! If you are unhappy, then lean into that unhappiness! Discover your anger about it! Make a point to look at your disappointment, sadness, and frustration. By allowing yourself to feel the reality of the situation, you will find the motivation to make changes. This is Principle #1: Despise Your Current Situation.

Yes, you can look for the positive aspects. Yes, you can focus on positive affirmations. And yes, you can think positively about the outcome. But are these motivating you to take action? Probably not. You need the balance of looking forward and honoring the positive aspects of yourself, your life, and your situation, but don't let them bury you in denial with the reality of your situation. If your situation needs to be changed, then use your anger or disappointment to fuel yourself into action.

Just because you have a 'negative' emotion about something, doesn't mean you will create a horrible situation. It means there's something wrong with the situation that's calling you to take action! Niju Kun #3, states that "one who practices Karate <u>must</u> follow the way of justice". This means that you cannot sit back in denial where unjust actions are unfolding...especially your own.

Angie

The Black Belt Money Master

www.blackbeltmoneymaster.com

Appendix A

Secrets Of the Wise

Astangas:

1. Yamas (moral restraints)
   - Ahimsa (non-violence)
   - Satya (truthfulness)
   - Asteya (non-stealing)
   - Brahmacharya (proper sexual conduct)
   - Aparagraha (non-possessiveness)
2. Niyamas (observances)
   - Saucha (purity, cleanliness)
   - Santosha (contentment)
   - Tapa (austerity)
   - Svadhyaya (study)
   - Ishvara Pranidhana (self-surrender/devotion to God)
3. Asana (physical practices)
4. Pranayama (breath control)
5. Pratyahara (sense withdrawal)
6. Dharana (concentration)
7. Dhyana (meditation)
8. Samadhi (absorption)

Appendix B

The Four Noble Truths

1. Dhuka (living is suffering)
2. Trishna/Raga (the cause of suffering is craving/desire)
3. Nirodha (suffering can stopped)
4. The Eight Fold Path (the path to stop suffering)

The Eight Fold Path

1. Samma Ditthi (right understanding)
2. Samma Sankappa (right thought)
3. Samma Vaca (right speech)
4. Samma Kammanta (right action)
5. Samma Ajiva (right livelihood)
6. Samma Vayama (right effort)
7. Samma Sati (right mindfulness)
8. Samma Samadhi (right concentration)

References...

Secrets Of the Wise

The Patanjali Yoga Sutras

- The Yoga Sutras of Patanjali, by Edwin Bryant
- The Science of Yoga, by L.K. Taimni
- The Yoga Sutras, by Nicolai Bachman

The Bhagavad Gita

- Introduced and translated by Eknath Easwaran

Shotokan Karate's Dojo Kun and Niju Kun

- Seek Perfection of Character, the Guiding Principals for the Martial Arts & Everyday Living, by Teruyuki Okasaki

Zen & Buddism

- The Complete Book of Zen, Wong Kiew Kit

About the author…

Angie Marie Grainger, CPA /PFS, CFP®, and Certified Money Coach is the Founder of RETHINK Money Coaching, Inc. and a BLACK-BELT Money Coaching Expert at helping people master their money and discovering their ideal lives.

Angie is a highly passionate, inspiring speaker and leader in delivering innovative, do-able, methods of teaching money concepts and thinking differently about money. Not only as an author and speaker, but her passion and enthusiasm are also captured in her on-line video coaching programs and social media.

Angie is a Distinguished Graduate of Sonoma State University's School of Business and Economics, and Outstanding Graduate Student from Golden Gate University with her Master's Degree in Taxation and Financial Planning.

Angie is influential to other CPAs and financial advisors through her leadership as Vice-Chair of the California Society of CPAs State Financial Planning Committee, as well as in helping build regional prosperity through financial education as past-Chair of the State Financial Literacy Committee.

Angie is a Black Belt in Shotokan Karate and consistently pursues her study of eastern philosophy.

BLACK BELT MONEY MASTER

FOCUS · DISCIPLINE · MASTERY

Angie M. Grainger, CPA/PFS, CFP®, Certified Money Coach, and Black Belt in Shotokan Karate

www.blackbeltmoneymaster.com

Made in the USA
Monee, IL
09 November 2026

67971933R00026